Worcester County Maryland

Administrators Bonds and Inventories

1783-1790

Ruth T. Dryden

HERITAGE BOOKS
2007

HERITAGE BOOKS
AN IMPRINT OF HERITAGE BOOKS, INC.

Books, CDs, and more—Worldwide

For our listing of thousands of titles see our website
at
www.HeritageBooks.com

Published 2007 by
HERITAGE BOOKS, INC.
Publishing Division
65 East Main Street
Westminster, Maryland 21157-5026

Copyright © 1989 Ruth Dryden

Other books by the author:
Cementary Records Worcester County Maryland
Cemetary Records Somerset County Maryland
Land Records of Somerset County Maryland
Parish of Somerset: Records of Somerset County Maryland
Rent Rolls of Somerset County Maryland 1663-1723
Stepney Parish Records of Somerset County Maryland

All rights reserved. No part of this book may be reproduced or transmitted in any form or by any means, electronic or mechanical, including photocopying, recording or by any information storage and retrieval system without written permission from the author, except for the inclusion of brief quotations in a review.

International Standard Book Number: 978-1-58549-491-0

WORCESTER COUNTY MARYLAND
Administrators bonds and inventories- 1783-1790

ADKINS, Stephen, 11 Oct 1786, bonds by
John Adkins adm., George Adkins adm., Bartholomew Slattery
Inventory- John and George Adkins exec. signed by Atkins Dennis

ADKINS, Stanton, 1 Sep.1790 bonds by
Milly Adkins, Joseph Adkins, Ayres Parker
Inventory-Milly Adkins exec., next of kin- Meddleton Adkins, George Adkins

ALLEN, Joshua, 20 Mar 1785, bonds by
Sophia Allen exec, Elijah Sturgis, Laban Hudson
Inventory-Sophia Allen adminx. signed by Stephen Allen, William Holland, John Allen Sr. Selby Newton

ALLEN, Joseph, 16 Aug 1753, bonds by
Henry Franklin, James Martin, James Round Morris
Inventory-Henry Franklin exec. no kin listed

ALLEN, Euphemia, 24 Jun 1786, bonds by
Josiah Mitchell, Peter Chaille, William Purnell
(Joshua Mitchell exec. of Mrs. Euphama Allens will renounces administration (sick and Old.)
Inventory-(late wife of William Allen Esq) Joshua Mitchell Esq, exec. next of kin-William Purnell, Ann Dennis

ANDERSON, Nathan, 12 Oct 1787 bonds by
Nancy Anderson, Zorababel Maddux, Lemuel Franklin
Inventory-Nancy Anderson adminx. no kin listed

ANDREWS, Littleton, bonds by, 22 Aug 1783
Peggy Andrews, William Parker, Turvill Mumford
Inventory- Peggy Andrews Admx. next of kin Ansello Andrews, Caleb White

ATKINSON, Angelo, 27 Mar 1789 bonds by
Comfort Atkinson, Benjamin Dennis Esq, Francis Randall
Inventory- Comfort Atkinson exec., next of kin Thomas Atkinson, James Atkinson

ATKINSON, William, 30 Jun 1784 bonds by
Sarah Atkinson admx., John Ennalls, Peter Chaille Esq.
Inventory- Sarah Atkinson adm., next of kin Angelo Atkinson and James Atkinson

ATKINSON, John 4 July 1783 Inventory.
came Levin Blake who married Mary Atkinson execurtix

AUSTIN, Mathias, 21Nov1787, bonds by
John Austin, Elijah Shockley, John Richardson
Inventory-John Austin exec., next of kin Ann Maglammry and Betey Austin

AYRES, Henry, 28 Jan 1786 bonds by
Rachel Ayres, John Ayres, John Johnson
Inventory- Rachel Ayres admx. next of kin James Ayres and Matthew Hopkins

AYRES,Francis, 7 Feb 1784 bonds by
    (Benjamin Tull & Leah Tull renounces adm. to Henry Ayres)
    Henry Ayres, Matthew Hopkins, George Martin
    Inventory- Adm. Henry Ayres next of kin John Selby
    and Zadock Selby

AYRES, Francis 20 Aug 1786, bonds by
    Rachel Ayres adm., Jonathan Stevenson,James Stevenson

BALL,John, 1 Jan 1790 bonds by
    Rhoda Townsend Ball admx.,Joshua Townsend Esq.,Major White
    Inventory-came Rhoda Townsend Toadvine late Rhoda Townsend
    Ball admx. and Joshua Townsend adm. next of kin John Ball
    and Anne Ball

BALLARD,Samuel, 2 Mar 1790 bonds by
    Ballard Blades,Levi Houston, Bayley Young

BASSITT,Jemmia, 23 Oct 1789 bonds by
    William Bassitt,Cornelius Morris,Jeremiah Townsend
    Inventory-William Bassitt exec. next of kin John
    Bassitt and William Bassett

BULY,Phillip, 8 Mar 1786 bonds by
    Titus Buly,James Bruington,Elijah Shockley
    Inventory-Titus Buley adm.,next of kin, negros Sylvea
    Briley and Esther Briley

BELL,Henry, 13 Nov 1786 bonds by
    Molley Bell,Isaac Ayres,Thomas Dale
    Inventory-Molley Bell exec. next of kin Sally Townsend
    and Christian Hazzard

BELL,William, 18 Feb 1787 bonds by
    Levin Bell adm.,Alexander McAllen,Robert Slocomb

BENNETT,William, 14 Nov 1787 bonds by
    Rebecca Bennett,Samuel Tarr, Levin Sturgis
    Inventory-Rebecca Bennett exec. no kin listed

BETHARDS,Samuel 11 Jul 1783, bonds by
    Elizabeth Bethards,Charles Parker,Barkley Townsend
    Inventory-Eliza Bethards adm.,next of kin Elizabeth
    Bethards and William Jarman Bethards

BETTS,Robert, 23 April 1784 bonds by
    Mary Betts, McKemmie Hudson,John Rackliffe
    Inventory-28 Jul 1787 Isaac Savage and Mary his wife
    adminx., next of kin,Nehemiah Benson,Nancy Betts

BEVANS,John, 2 Dec 1783, bonds by
    Nelly Bevans,James Tull, Jonathan Tull,McKimmy Porter
    Inventory- James Tull adm.21 May 1784 next of kin,
    Jemima Bevans,Henrietta Bevans

BISHOP,Smith, 3 Aug 1783 bonds by
    Peter Chaille,Benjamin Purnell, Hannah Bishop
    Inventory-Hannah Bishop adminx., next of kin Sarah
    Hayward, Charlotte Martin

BLADES,Samuel, 9 Oct 1783 bonds by
    Millicent Blades admx.,William Merrill,Littleton Long
    Inventory-Millicent Blades,exec., next of kin-Jehug
    Blades,Samuel Blades

BLADES,Samuel 28 May 1790
Inventory- Ballard Blades adm., next of kin Milly
Blades, Gatta Blades

BOSTON,Naboth, 5 Aug 1785, bonds by
Sarah Boston,Benjamin Hudson,Robert Melvin
Inventory- Sarah Boston adm.,next of kin Daniel Boston
and Levinah Coner

BOSTON,Jacob, 5 Dec 1788 bonds by
Esau Boston,Isaac Boston,James Henderson
Inventory-Esau Boston exec., next of kin, Isaac Boston
and Jacob Boston

BOWEN,Rackliffe 15 Jan 1787 bonds by
(Luke Bowen renounces administration) William
Stevenson,Isaac Hill, Robert Martin
Inventory-Wm.Stevenson adm., next of kin, Jethro Bowen
and Zadock Selby

BOWEN,Levin, 13 Mar 1787 bonds by
Rachel Bowen,John Bowen,William Bowen
Inventory-Rachel Bowen adminx.,next of kin-David Bowen,
Salathiel Bowen

BOWEN,Whittington, 10 Apr 1790 bonds by
Whittington Bowen,James Bowen,Peal Franklin
Inventory-Whittington Bowen exec.,James Bowen exec.
next of kin-William F.Bowen, Sarah Morris

BOWEN,John, 15 Oct 1784 bonds by
(Jethro Bowen,John Bowen,Luke Bowen & William Bowen rejects
adm.) Jessee Bowen adm.,Robert Hudson,John Truitt Jr.

BRASHURE,William, 27 Sep 1784 bonds by
(Sarah Brasher widow rejects adm.) Belitha Brashure adm.,
Israel Townsend, Samuel Johnson
Inventory-Belitha Brasher adm.,next of kin, Ann Brasher
and Godfrey Brasher

BRATTEN,Joseph 13 Feb 1783 bonds by
Ann Brattan adm.,Hampton Hopkins adm.,Samuel Johnson
John Kerby
Inventory-Hampton Hopkins Surviving adm. 4 Jun 1789
next of kin-Wilson Brattan, John Scarborough

BRATTEN,Ann, 26 Dec 1788 bonds by
Hillary Pitts,Belitha Powell,John Taylor
Inventory-Hillary Pitts exec.,next of kin, John Scarborough,
and John Selby

BRAVARD,Adam, 15 Jan 1783 bonds by
Benjamin Hudson exec., William Ironshire,John Postly
Inventory-Nenjamin Hudson exec., next of kin Thomas
Hudson and Solomon Hudson

BREWINGTON,John, 20 Oct 1786 bonds by
John Brewington,James Perdue,Spencer Davis
Inventory- John Bruington adm. next of kin, Smith
Brewington, James Brewington

BRITTINGHAM,Samuel, 6 Jun 1787 bonds by
Joseph Richardson,William Corbin,William Bevans
Inventory-Wm.Bevans adm. next of kin, William Brittingham Sr
William Brittingham Jr.

BRITTINGHAM,Isaac, 30 Jun 1786 Inventory
    Jeptha Brittingham exec. signed by William Brittingham
    and Samuel Brittingham
BRITTINGHAM,Pointer, 11 Nov 1773 Inventory
    Belitha Brittingham adm.(16 Jul 1786) signed by William
    Brittingham and Samuel Brittingham
BRITTINGHAM,Peggy 8 Aug 1788 Inventory
    Belitha Brittingham adm. next of kin-James Duer, McKimmy
    Porter. ments;legacies to Belitha Brittingham. Whereas
    the estate was appraised 15 yrs ago and was blended
    with her dec'd husbands Isaac Brittingham's estate, this
    inventory is now necessary. No kin listed
BRITTINGHAM,William 18 Sep 1789 bonds by
    Thomas Cottingham,Robert Richardson,Henry G. Willitt
BROWN,George 27 Jun 1787 bonds by
    Sarah Brown,William Wilson,George Brown
    Inventory- Sarah Brown exec., next of kin William Sloth,
    Andrew Brown
CAHOON, Ephraim 12 Oct 1790 Inventory,
    Joseph Green adm., no kin known
CAIN-John 12 Aug 1788 bonds by
    Nancy Cain admx.,James Selby,Isaac Boston
    Inventory-Nancy cain admx.,next of kin Joseph Merrill,
    William Venneretson
CANNON,John 24 Jun 1786 bonds by
    (unadministered by Sarah Cannon now dec'd)
    Josiah Mitchell,William Handy,Benjamin Purnell of Walton
CAMPBELL,Ebenezer 10 Feb 1786 bonds by
    Samuel Hopkins Round adm.,Solomon Long,Edward Vandome
CAMPBELL,Ebenezer 19 Dec 1788 bonds by
    Joshua Townsend,Thomas Jones,Samuel H. Round
CAREY,Levin 11 Nov 1783 bonds by
    John Townsend,William Noble, Levin Carey exec.
    Inventory- Levin Carey exec. next of kin William Williams,
    Leah Carey
CAREY,Justice 6 Apr 1786 bonds by
    Josiah Robinson,Henderson Robinson,Levi Robinson
    Inventory- Josiah Robinson adm.next of kin, Levi Carey,
    Ann Townsend
CHRISTOPHER,Elizabeth 15 Jun 1787 bonds by
    George Teague,William Dreaden,James Givan
    Inventory-George Teague adm.,next of kin Isaac Savage,
    Hannah Christopher
CLARK,Garshon 14 Jun 1783 bonds by
    Lyddal Clark,Elijah Timmons,Jessee Holloway
CLOGG,Samuel 6 Feb 1787 bonds by
    (Hafter Clogg rejects adm. of fathers est.)
    William Stephen Hill, Nathaniel Davis,Matthew Davis
COE,Asa, 9 May 1787 bonds by
    Solomon Perkins,John Perkins,William Stevenson
    Inventory- Solomon Perkins adm. next of kin John Coe,
    Avery Coe

COLLINS,Parker 4 Sep 1786 bonds by
    Dennis Hudson adm.,William Undrill, Outten Truitt
    Inventory- Dennis Hudson adm. next of kin Parker Selby
    and John Selby

COLLINS,John 12 Jun 1786 bonds by
    Mary Collins adm.,Eli Hudson,Dennis Hudson,Edward Hammond
    of Edward
    Inventory-Eli Hudson,Mary Collins adm. next of kin
    Parker Selby and Jessee Selby

COLLINS,Esther 12 May 1786 bonds by
    Mary Collins adm.Eli Hudson Adm. Dennis Hudson, Edward
    Hammond of Edward
    Inventory-Mary Collins & Eli Hudson adms., next of kin,
    Parker Selby and Jessee Selby

COLLINS,Solomon, 21 Aug 1789
    (Unadministered by Elizabeth Collins dec'd) Annanias
    Hudson,Josiah Mithcell, Edward Henry

CONNER,James, 29 Aug 1787 bonds b y
    James Low,Isaac Duncan, Zadock Selby(St.Martins)
    Inventory-James Laws exec. next of kin William Hook,
    Mary Hook

COOCKSAY,Priscilla 7 Jun 1786 bonds by
    Stephen Christopher adm.,Isaac Phillips,Somerset Downey

CORDRAY,Jonathan 12 Apr 1790 inventory
    Mary Cordray adm. next of kin, Abraham Cordray, Mary
    Cordray

COSTON,Ezekiel 7 Jan 1785 bonds by
    Ezekiel Coston,James Martin,Samuel Handy
    Inventory-exec.Ezekiel Coston, next of kin Josiah
    Dickeson, Mathias Coston

COSTON,John, 5 Dec 1787 bonds by
    Ezekiel Coston adm.,Col.James Martin,Col.William Handy
    Inventory-Ezekiel Coston adm., next of kin Mathias
    Coston,Jessee Dickerson

COTTINGHAM, 20 May 1785 Bonds by
    Betty Cottingham adm.,William Handy,Josiah Dickerson
    Inventory-Betty Cottingham extecx. next of kin Daniel
    Cottingham and Margaret Cottingham

CRAWFORD,William 2 Jan 1784 bonds by
    Polly Crawford exec.,Stephen Sturgis,Outten Sturgis
    Inventory-Polly Crawford exec., next of kin, Elijah
    Merrill, Comfort Merrill

CRAWFORD,John, 19 Mar 1784 bonds
    Polly Crawford adm, Stephen Sturgis, Henry Ayres

CRAWFORD,Rachel 19 Mar 1784 bonds by
    Polly Crawford adm, Stephen Sturgis,Henry Ayres

CROPPER,Levi 3 Mar 1786 bonds by
    Reuben Cropper,Esau Williams, Matthew Hopkins
    Inventory- Reuben Cropper adm., next of kin Nathaniel
    Cropper and Bela Cropper

CROPPER,Nathaniel 7 Apr 1787 bonds by
  Reuben Cropper,Rouse Fassitt,George Stevenson
  Inventory-Reuben Cropper adm., next of kin, Luke
  Cropper and Edmond Cropper Jr.

CROPPER,Jessee 9 Mar 1784 bonds by
  (Susan Cropper renounces adm.) Reuben Cropper adm.,
  James Purnell, Matthew Hopkins
  Inventory- Reuben Cropper adm. next of kin Noble Cropper
  and Nathaniel Cropper Sr.

CROPPER,Jessee 27 Mar 1787 bonds by
  Isabiah Cropper adm.,Annanias Warren, Annanias Jarman
  Esau Williams, Thomas Warren
  Inventory-Isabiah Cropper adm. next of kin, Bela
  Cropper and Reuben Cropper

CURREN,John, 20 Feb 1785 bonds by
  Caleb Tingle, Benjamin McCormack,Sarah Curren
  Inventory-26 Jan 1786, Josiah Mitchell adm.,no kin listed

DALE,John, 13 Jan 1787 bonds by
  Tabitha Dale exec.,Thomas Dale, Seth Whaley
  Inventory-Tabitha Dale exec, next of kin Thomas Dale
  and Joseph Evans

DASHIELL,Joseph 13 Jan 1787 bonds by
  (Susanna Dashiell rejects adm. of husband's est.)
  Benjamin Dashiell, John Done,Peter Chaille, William
  Purnell(of Croppers Neck)

DAVIS,Ann, 29 Feb 1788 bonds by
  Nixon Davis exec.,Selby Parker,John Parker
  Inventory-Nixon Davis,exec. next of kin Matthias Davis
  and Sarah Davis

DAVIS,Edward, 21 Mar 1788 bonds by
  (Rhoda Davis exec. rejects adm. to son Thomas)
  Thomas Davis exec, Benjamin Davis,James Parker
  Inventory-Thomas Davis exec. signed by Benjamin Davis,
  Samuel Davis,Solomon Davis, Margaret Fassitt

DAVIS,John, 19 Jul 1783 bonds by
  John Davis adm.,Robert Schoolfield,Rownd Givans
  Inventory-John Davis adm. next of kin Mary Reed, Nixon Davis

DAVIS,John 14 Sep 1789 bonds by
  Clear Trowor Davis adm.,John Flint,William Bigland
  Inventory-Clear trower Davis adm. next of kin Tabby Davis,
  Reuben Davis

DAVIS,Levin, 26 Mar 1784 bonds by
  Rachel Davis exec.,Matthew Davis,William Purnell,Littleton
  Robins
  Inventory-Rachel Davis exec. next of kin, Mary Jones,
  Belitha Brittingham. 9 Oct 1787 came Martha Davis acting exec

DAVIS,Samuel 27 Mar 1775 inventory
  adm.Sinah Davis 8 Jun 1784 next of kin Edward Davis,
  Benjamin Davis

DAVIS,Saul- 9 Nov 1787 bonds by
  Edward Hammond exec.,Jessee Bennett,Richard Hall
  Inventory-Edw.Hammond exec.,next of kin Edward Hammond,
  Elizabeth Hammond

DAVIS,Solomon 14 Mar 1784 bonds by
    (Elizabeth Davis widow accepts will of husband)
    John Davis exec., William Morris,Holland Smock
    Inventory-John Davis exec.,next of kin Thomas Purnell,
    James Wilson

DAVIS,Truitt, 18 Jan 1788 bonds by
    Betty Davis adm.,Phillip Davis,William Davis
    Inventory-Betty Davis adm., next of kin,Levi Davis,
    Vilett Davis

DAVIS,Patience-20 Ovt 1786 bonds by
    Spencer Davis,John Brewington,William Willis
    Inventory-Spencer Davis adm. next of kin,John Davis
    and Elijah Davis

DAVIS,Thomas, 26 Dec 1788 bonds by
    Martha Davis, Belitha Powell,John Postly

DAVIS,William 15 May 1777 Inventory
    exec.Joshua Davis, next of kin Truitt Davis,Levi Davis

DASHIELL,Joseph,Col. 1 Mar 1787 Inventory
    Benjamin Frederick Augustus Ceasar Dashiell acting adm.
    next of kin-Susannah Dashiell, William Pitts Dashiell

DENNIS,Henry 26 Oct 1785 bonds by
    Ann Dennis adm.,Samuel Handy adm.,William Allen, William
    Purnell
    Inventory-Ann Dennis and Samuel Handy adm. next of
    kin, John Dennis & Robert Dennis

DENNIS,Littleton 13 Dec 1784 bonds by
    John Teackle adm. of Accoc.Co.Va.,Henry Dennis adm.,
    Southy Whittington, John Marshall

DENNIS,Susanna 13 Dec 1784 bonds by
    John Teackle of Accoc.Co.Va.,Henry Dennis,Southy Whittington,
    John Marshall
    Inventory-John Teackle surv.adm. next of kin,Elizabeth
    Teackle and Sarah Waters

DICKESON,Nehemiah 11 Jan 1785 bonds by
    (Betty Dickeson renounces administration)
    James Dickeson,Littleton Long,William Merrill
    Inventory-James Dickerson adm. next of kin,William
    Milbourn,Francis Houston

DICKERSON,Joshua 17 Jan 1783 bonds by
    Jonah Dickerson adm.,Thomas Barns,Joseph Tilghman

DISHERSOON,George 26 Oct 1784 bonds by
    George Disharoon adm.,John Cathell,Thomas Fooks

DISHEROON,George 6 Mar 1789 bonds by
    Stephen Disheroon exec.,William Townsend,Henry Toadvine
    Inventory-Stephen Disheroon exec.,next of kin,Constant
    Disheroon,Stephen Disheroon Sr.

DIXON,Isaac 10 Oct 1782 Inventory
    Adm.Frances Dixon. next of kin David Dixon,Ambrose Dixon

DONE, Robert 28 Jan 1785 bonds by
    Peter Chaille Sr, John Done, Isaac Houston, Willima Purnell
DONOWAY, Thomas 12 Nov 1784 bonds by
    Nancy Donoway, William Baker, George Lewis
    9 Aug 1785 William Baker, Isaac Purnell, Josiah Mitchell
    whereas Wm. Baker and George Lewis was bound with Nancy
    Donoway admx. of Thomas who hath since intermarried
    with Joseph Richardson late of Worc.Co. now deceased.
    William Baker now adm.
DRYDEN, Joshua 26 Aug 1785 bonds
    Sarah Dryden adm., William Handy (Noswattix) Daniel
    Cottingham
    Inventory- Sarah Dryden admx. next of kin Elias Benston
    and Samuel Dryden 2 Nov 1787 came William McDaniel and
    Sarah his wife exectx.
DRYDEN, John, 28 Aug 1789 bonds by
    Moses Dryden, Levi Holland, George Purnell
    Inventory-Moses Dryden exec. next of kin Samuel and
    William Dryden
DRYDEN, William 22 Dec 1789 bonds by
    (Samuel Dryden Sr, Isaac Dryden rejects adm. to Thomas
    Dryden)
    Thomas Dryden adm., Samuel Dryden, Isaac Dryden
    Inventory of William Dryden son of Samuel-Thomas Dryden
    adm. next of kin-Samuel Dryden and Samuel Dryden Jr.
DUNCAN, Levin, 28 Nov 1788 bonds by
    Molly Duncan Hammond, Parker Selby (Buckingham)
    Inventory-Molley Duncan exec., next of kin, Josiah
    Duncan and Charles" Duncan
ELLISON, Luke 13 Jan 1787 bonds by
    Rhoda Ellison, Nehemiah Latchum, Jessee Davis
    Inventory-Rhoda Ellison exec., next of kin, Laban Taylor,
    Joshua Taylor
ESHAM, Joseph 6 Feb 1784 bonds by
    Thomas Layfield, John Layfield, William Holland
EVANS, Gammage 10 Nov 1783 bonds by
    Martha Evans exec., Walton Purnell, Benjamin McCormack
    Inventory, exec. Martha Evans next of kin, Zeno Evans,
    Powell Evans
EVANS, Sarah 4 Jan 1788 bonds by
    Rhoda Evans, Levi Mills, Thomas Dale
    Inventory-George Parker and Rhoda his wife exectx. next
    of kin-John Evans and Isaac Evans
FALCONER, William 5 Mar 1788 bonds by
    Charles Taylor, Joseph Green, John Prideix
    Inventory-Charles Taylor adm., next of kin, Eleanor Falconer
FALL, Levi, 8 Mar 1786 bonds by
    Samuel Johnson, Solomon Baker, James Waters
    Inventory-James Waters adm. next of kin, Kendall Kennett
FAREWELL, John 13 Jan 1787 bonds by
    Anna Farewell exec, Francis Wharton exec. Benjamin Quillen,
    Samuel Lockwood
    Inventory-Anne Farewell, Frances Wharton execs. next of kin,
    Sophia Stevens, Leirner Tubbs

FASSITT, David 31 Dec 1784 bonds by
Margaret Fassitt, William Purnell, James Martin
Inventory-Margaret Fassitt exec. next of kin-William
Fassitt and Peter Collyer

FASSITT, John 28 Aug 1787, bonds by
Mary Fassitt, Charles Rackliffe, Rouse Fassitt
Inventory-Mary Fassitt exec., next of kin, John Fassitt,
James Fassitt, Elijah Fassitt

FASSITT, John 6 Feb 1789 bonds by
Charles Rackliffe, James Fassitt, Jessee Jones, James Parker
(unadministered by Mary Fassitt since dead)
(William Fassitt renounces adm. of fathers estate and
administration of Mother Mary's estate 19 Jan 1789)

FASSITT, Mary 6 Feb 1789 bonds by
Charles Rackliffe, James Fassitt, Jessee Jones, James Parker
Inventory-James Fassitt and Charles Rackliffe adms.
next of kin-Elijah and Rouse Fassitt

FASSITT, William 1 Jun 1786 bonds by
William Fassitt, Joshua Hodge, John Richards
Inventory-William Fassitt exec. next of kin, Peter
Collyer and Thomas Selby

FERGUSON, John 5 Sep 1783 bonds by
Samuel Hopkins Rounds adm., John Pope Mitchell, Joseph Miller
Inventory-Samuel Hopkins Round adm. no kin listed

FINCH, George 19 Aug 1790 inventory
Ebe Finch admx., next of kin, Sarah Finch, Betty Finch

FREEMAN, Moses, 29 Jun 1789 bonds by
Mary Freeman, Michael Freeman, William Bainum
Inventory-Mary Freeman exec. Michael Freeman exec.
next of kin-Joseph and William Freeman

FREENEY, William 27 Sep 1786 bonds by
Anne Freeney adm., Hezekiah Maddux, Daniel Melson
Inventory-Ann Freeney adm. next of kin, John Freeney
and Joshua Freeney

GILLETT, Sarah 25 Oct 1784 bonds by
William Polk adm., Joshua Riggin, Joshua Townsend
Inventory-William Polk Adm. next of kin, Richard Rowley,
Eleanor Dickerson

GLADIN, Joseph 14 May 1784 bonds by
Rachel Gladin admx., Samuel Ingorsol, Levin Carey
Inventory- Rachel Gladden admx., next of kin, Samuel
Ingersol, Richard Ingersol

GLADSTON, Thomas 15 Feb 1788 bonds by
William Davis adm., Zadock Sturgis, John Bishop
Inventory-William Davis adm. next of kin, Saley Webb
and Hanner Webb

GODFREY, Joseph 26 Apr 1784 bonds by
Jemima Godfrey, William Townsend, Benjamin McCormack
Inventory- no kin listed

GORDY,Ellinor 4 Nov 1788 bonds by
    William Gordy exec.,John Gordy,Daniel Melson
    Inventory-William Gordy,exec. next of kin, Daniel
    Melson and Levy King

GORDY,Peter 14 Mar 1788 bonds by
    Eleanor Gordy Admx, William Gordy,John Parker, Samuel Fern
    Inventory-Eleanor Gordy and William Gordy admins.
    next of Kin-Nathan Gordy, John Gordy
    2 Mar 1790 William Gordy surviving adm.

GORNWELL,John 28 May 1784 bonds by
    Mary Gornwell adm.,Robert Schoolfield,Nathaniel Bratten
    Inventory-Mary Gornwell adm. next of kin, Major Gornwell
    and Elizabeth Bishop

GRAY,Jacob 21 Dec 1784 bonds by
    Wise Gray exec.,Nehemiah Dorman,Robert Martin Richardson
    Inventory-Wise Gray ex., next of kin, Sarah Spencer,
    Elizabeth Christopher

GREEN,Ephraim, 12 Jun 1789 bonds by
    Joseph Green, Hillary Pitts, Mijah Davis

GRIFFEN,William 27 Jan 1786 bonds by
    Edward Hammond of Edward adm.,George Truitt,Major Townsend
    Inventory-Edward Hammond adm., next of kin, Belitha
    Griffith, Milbe Griffin

GUTHREY,Joshua 24 Oct 1788 bonds by
    John Selby Esq, Nancy Williams exec.,John Outten Sturgiss
    Inventory-Nancy Williams exec., next of kin, William
    Guthery and Joshua Guthrey

HALL,Catherine 11 Mar 1785 bonds by
    James Godfrey adm.,William White,Jessee Bennett
    Inventory-James Godfrey exec., signed by James Mumford
    and James Godfrey

HAMMOND,Zedekiah 2 Nov 1787 bonds by
    Leah Hammond exec, Edward Hammond Jr.,Samuel Davis
    Inventory-Leah Hammond exec., next of kin, Joshua
    Hammond and Edward Hammond

HANDY,Benjamin 15 Feb 1788 Inventory
    Capt Thomas Martin adm., next of kin, J.A. Handy, and
    Levin Handy

HANDY,Elizabeth 5 Mar 1787 bonds by
    (James Handy relinquishes adm. to bro.Levin Handy)
    Levin Handy adm., Jonathan Hutcheson,Peter Chaille Jr.

HANDY,John 2 Apr 1788 additional inventory
    Capt Thomas Martin adm.

HARRISON,Erasmus 13 Nov 1786 bonds by
    (Mary Harrison exec. of Erasmus rejects adm.)
    Erasmus Harrison exec.,Thomas Dale,Isaac Ayres
    Inventory-Erasmus Harrison exec., next of kin, Seth
    Harrison and Tabby Harrison

HAYMAN,Isaac 6 Oct 1784 bonds by
    Rebecca Hayman adm.,John Hayman,Charles Hayman Jr.
    Inventory-Rebecca Hayman adm., next of kin, Stephen
    Bain, Charles Hayman

HAYMAN, Charles 9 Jun 1789 bonds by
   Sarah Hayman exec., John Hayman of John, Samuel Carey
   Inventory-Sarah Hayman adm., next of kin, Revel Hayman
   and James Hayman

HAYWARD, John 20 Jul 1787 bonds by
   Paul Hayward exec., William Hayward, John Miller
   Inventory-Paul Hayward exec., next of kin John Hayward
   and William Hayward

HEATHER, John 20 Jul 1787 bonds by
   Ellinor Heather exec., Jessee Jones, William Purnell Esq.
   of Croppers Neck
   Inventory-Elinor Heather admx., next of kin Eleanor
   Mumford, Handy Heather

HENDERSON, Benjamin 13 May 1790 inventory
   Elizabeth Henderson adm., next of kin, John Henderson,
   Mary Lambden

HENDERSON, Isaac 23 Sep 1784 bonds by
   Esther Henderson admx., Benjamin Holland, Charles Bennett
   Inventory-Esther Henderson adm. next of kin, Brittingham
   Henderson and William Henderson

HENDERSON, Ephraim 23 Jul 1785 bonds by
   Tabitha Henderson admx, John Johnson, John Fleming
   Inventory-Tabitha Henderson exec. next of kin, Brittingham
   Henderson and William Henderson
   10 Sep 1788 came Tabitha Selby late Tabitha Henderson

HENDERSON, Jessee 15 Feb 1787 bonds by
   (Rhody Bond rejects adm. to son Brittingham Henderson
   and he also rejects adm.)
   William Beavan Henderson adm, William Bennett, William
   Stephen Hill
   Inventory-William Henderson Adm. signed by Brittingham
   Henderson and Mary Brittingham

HENDERSON, Levin 29 Mar 1789 bonds by
   Curtis Henderson exec, John Jones, Elijah Laws
   Inventory- Curtis Henderson exec., next of kin Jessee
   Henderson and Nancy Henderson

HILL, Johnson 2 Oct 1786 bonds by
   William Stephen Hill, John Ayres, Moses Chaille

HILL, Rebecca 15 Mar 1788 bonds by
   William Parker, Mary Parker his wife, Nancy Hill,
   Henry Parker, William Selby of Snow Hill.
   Inventory-18 Mar 1788, William Parker and Nancy Laws
   (late Nancy Hill) execs. next of kin, Isaac Hill, Isaac
   Evans

HILL, Stephen 20 Dec 1784 bonds by
   Zipporah Hill exec., Schoolfield Parker, Isaac Hill
   next of kin, Isaac Hill, William Hill

HILL, William 8 Sep 1787 bonds by
   Elizabeth Hill exec., Josiah Mitchell, Henry Franklin
   Inventory-Elizabeth Hill exec., next of kin Isaac Hill
   and William Stephen Hill

HOLLAND,Levin 18 May 1789 bonds by
    Esther Holland,exec.,Patrick Waters,Elisha Purnell of Matthew
    Inventory-Esther Holland exec. next of kin Michael Holland and William Holland

HOLLAND,William 30 May 1786 bonds by
    William Holland exec.,William Stephen Hill,John Ayres

HOLLAND,William 18 Nov 1786 bonds by
    Levi Holland adm.,Edmund Cropper,Patrick Waters

HOLLOWAY,John 2 Mar 1789 bonds by
    (Armwell Long rejects administration)
    John Dennis,John Tull,Abisha Davis
    Inventory-John Dennis acting exec. next of kin, Ely Holloway(her mark, Mary Hudson

HOSHIER,John 20 Mar 1783 bonds by
    Levinah Hoshier adm.,Henry Parker,William Parker

HORSEY,Stephen 30 Sep 1788 bonds by
    George Livingston,Levi Cathell,Moses Parke
    Inventory-George Livingstone exec. next of kin, Sarah and Sarah Livingston

HOUSTON,Jehu 20 May 1772 inventory
    Mary Houston adm., next of kin James Houston and Mary Houston
    13 Jun 1784 came James Stevenson and Mary his wife adminx. of Jehu Houston

HUDSON,John 14 Feb 1783 bonds by
    Rachel Hudson, William Ironshire,John FAssitt

HUDSON,John 2 May 1783 bonds by
    Esther Hudson adm.,Solomon Walton,Samuel Handy

HUDSON,Martha 3 Mar 1788 bonds by
    Jessee Hudson, John Wright, Jessee Selby

HUDSON,Samuel 22 Jul 1785 bonds by
    Liza Hudson,William Bennett, Joshua Guthrey
    Inventory-Liza Hudson admx., next of kin, Laban Hudson and Moses Hudson

HUDSON,Solomon 29 May 1786 bonds by
    Esther Hudson exec., Caleb Tingle,William Stevenson
    Inventory-Esther Hudson exec. next of kin, Annanias Hudson and John Hudson

IRONSHIRE,Isaac 15 Oct 1784 bonds by
    William Underhill adm.,Esther Underhill, Nehemiah Dorman
    Inventory-Wm.Undrill adm. next of kin, Mary Evans, Esther Ironshire

IRONSHIRE,Sarah 18 Nov 1786 bonds by
    Henry Franklin,William Fassitt, Rouse Fassitt
    Inventory- Henry Franklin adm. next of kin,Eleanor Franklin and Alexander Franklin

IRONSHIRE,Joseph 28 Feb 1781, Inventory
    Esther Ironshire exec. next of kin, Benjamin Hudson, William Ironshire

IRONSHIRE,William 27 May 1786 bonds by
    Sarah Ironshire, Henry Franklin,John Postly

IRONSHIRE, William 10 Nov 1786 bonds by
    Henry Franklin adm., William Fassitt, Rouse Fassitt
    Inventory-Henry Franklin adm. next of kin, Isaac
    Ayres, John Bravard

JARMAN, Elijah 18 Jan 1788 bonds by
    James Parker exec., John Perkins, Thomas Jones
    Inventory-James Parker exec., next of kin, Henry
    Parker and Hillary Pitts

JARMAN, William 9 Jun 1785 bonds by
    Elijah Jarman adm., William Truitt, Peter Parker
    Inventory-Elijah Jarman adm.-next of kin, Margaret
    Porter and Rachel Jarman

JAVIN, John 17 Jan 1783 bonds by
    Benjamin Purnell adm., Levi Purnell, Wm. Stephen Hill

JOHNSON, Robert 3 Mar 1788 bonds by
    Patience Johnson execx., Hampton Hopkins, John Tindall
    Inventory-Patience Johnson exec. next of kin, Joseph
    Gray and Elizabeth Gray

JOHNSON, Lemuel 1 May 1784 bonds by
    Mary Johnson adm., Selby Parker, adm., Phillip Selby,
    Jacob Gray
    Inventory-Mary Johnson, Selby Parker adms., next of
    kin, John Johnson, James Johnson

JOHNSON, Samuel 10 Feb 1787 bonds by
    (Robert Johnson rejects administration)
    John Taylor adm., Isaac Purnell, John Richards
    Inventory-John Taylor adm. next of kin Robert Johnson
    and David Johnson

JOHNSON, John 25 Aug 1783 bonds by
    Thomas T. Johnson adm., Israel Townsend, Luke Townsend
    Inventory-Thomas Johnson adm. next of kin Peter Johnson
    and David Johnson

JOHNSON, Samuel 27 May 1786 bonds by
    Rachel Johnson, John Taylor, Robert Johnson

JOHNSON, Samuel 17 Nov 1784 bonds by
    Ader Johnson adm., William Merrill, James Quinton
    Inventory-Ador Johnson admx., next of kin, Purnell
    Brittingham and Samuel Johnson

JONES, John 9 Jun 1785 bonds by
    Sarah Jones adm. Esau Williams, Henry White
    Inventory-Sarah Townsend late Sarah Jones admx. 17 Aug 1787
    next of kin-Mary Williams, John Jones

JONES, George 8 Feb 1787 bonds by
    Bridget Jones, ex., Eli Truitt, William Hammond
    Inventory-Bridget Jones admx., next of kin, Jessee Jones
    and Thomas Jones

JONES, John 7 Nov 1788 bonds by
    Mary Jones, Annanias Bradford, Moses Chaille

JONES, Joseph 22 Apr 1783 bonds by
    William Jones exec., Bartholomew Slattery, Levi Smith
    Inventory-Wm. Jones exec. next of kin Joseph Jones and
    John Jones

JONES, William 11 April 1788 bonds by
    Giles Jones exec., John Jones Sr, John Jones of John

JONES,William 12 April 1788 inventory
    Giles Jones exec., next of kin, John Jones,Daniel Jones

KELLAM,James 10 Jul 1785 bonds by
    (Mary Kellam rejects administration of husband James)
    John Kellam adm.Joseph Kellam adm., Phillip Quinton
    Inventory-John Kellam,Joseph Kellam adms. next of kin,
    Rebecca Kellam, Tabitha Kellam

KENNITT,Kendal 13 Sep 1787 bonds by
    (Leah Kennitt rejects adm.widow of Kendal to Wm.Kennett)
    William Kennett adm.,Mathew Hopkins,Levin Hopkins
    Inventory-Wm.Kennett adm. next of kin,Eliabeth Kennett,
    Elizabeth Milbourn

KENNETT,Presgrave 15 Feb 1783 bonds by
    Susanna Kennett exec.,John Taylor,Hampton Hopkins
    Inventory-Susanna Kennett exec., next of kin,William
    Kennett,Mary Hopkins

KNOX,Nehemiah 18 Feb 1790 inventory
    Ezekiel Knox exec. next of kin Esther Roan,Solomon Knox

LAMBERSON, Thomas 11 Feb 1786 bonds by
    Leah Lamberson adm., John White
    Inventory-Leah Taylor,late Leah Lamberson,w/o George
    admx. 7 Apr 1787. next of kin, Richard Hall, William
    Sullivan

LAMBDEN,Thomas 13 Mar 1783 inventory
    James Atkinson exec., next of kin, James Atkinson
    and James Atkinson

LANE,Walter 12 Oct 1784 bonds by
    Leah Lane admx.,William Merrill,Walter Smith
    Inventory-Leah Lane admx., next of kin,William Lane,
    and Rachel Mills

LARREMORE,Elisha 25 Aug 1783 bonds by
    Rachel Larremore exec.,Benjamin McCormack,Reuben Cropper
    Inventory- Rachel Larremore, next of kin Reuben Cropper,
    Henry Smart?

LEWIS,Sarah 23 Aug 1783 bonds by
    David Fassitt adm., Annanias Hudson,Whittington Bowen

LONG,David 21 Jul 1783 bonds by
    Samuel Long,Edward Vandom, Henry White

LOWDEN,Thomas 20 Feb 1785 bonds by
    William Earger adm., Caleb Tingle,Joseph Mitchell
    Inventory- no kin

MADDUX,Lazarus 7 Jan 1785 bonds by
    Sophia Maddux admx.,John Drydden, Nehemiah Dorman
    Inventory-Sophia Maddux next of kin, Zerobabel Maddux,
    Merrill Maddux

MARCH,John 2 Mar 1784 bonds by
    Martha March adm.,John Perkins,Hillary Pitts
    Inventory-Martha March admx.,next of kin, Edward March,
    Elizabeth Curliss

MARCHMENT,Sterling 21 Feb 1783 bonds by
    Elizabeth Marchmant exec.,James Marchment exec.,William
    Selby
    Inventory-Elizabeth Marchment exec., next of kin,Levin
    Riley,Charles Marchment
MARCHMENT, Elizabeth 27 Jul 1790 Inventory
    Riley Marchment adm., next of kin Betsy Marchment and
    Dolla Marchment
MARSHALL,Esme 5 Oct 1784 bonds by
    (Thomas Marshall and John Marsahll rejects administration)
    George Marshall adm., Thomas Marshall, John Marshall
    Inventory-George Marshall adm., next of kin, Theophilius
    Marshall, Levin Marshall
MARTIN,Edward 10 Mar 1789 bonds by
    (Elizabeth Martin rejects adm)
    George Martin of Thomas, Thomas Martin Jr., Levin Martin
MARTIN,William 14 Aug 1784 inventory
    Exectx, Agnes Mills. next of kin Thomas Martin,James Martin
MASSEY,Hezekiah 21 Dec 1787 bonds by
    Selby Newton adm.,Parker Selby of Matthew, Selby Parker
    Inventory-Selby Newton adm. next of kin, Ann Massey,
    Ezekiah Johnson
MASSEY,Charity 27 Jun 1789 bonds by
    Henry Franklin, William Franklin, Peal Franklin
MASSEY,John 11 Feb 1786 bonds by
    Mary Massey,Caleb Tingle,Henry Franklin
    Inventory-Mary Massey exec., next of kin, John Fassitt,
    Elijah Fassitt
MEARS,John 2 Jan 1784 bonds by
    Sarah Mears adm.,James Perdue,Solomon Long
    Inventory-Sarah Mears adm., next of kin, Josiah Benson,
    Robert Benson
MELVIN,William 20 Feb 1784 bonds by
    William Melvin exec., James Phillips,John Melvin
    Inventory-Wm.Melvin exec., next of kin, Robert Melvin,
    Jonathan Melvin
MERRILL,Scarborough 3 Oct 1783 bonds by
    Sarah Merrill exec.,Josiah Merrill,Thomas Merrill
    Inventory- Sarah Merrill exec. next of kin, Thomas Merrill,
    Simpson Merrill
MERRILL,Levi 11 Feb 1785 bonds by
    Anne Merrill admx,John Bishop,Charles Bishop
    Inventory-Ann Merrill admx. next of kin,Arthur Merrill,
    Joseph Hudson,Sarah Boston 5 Dec 1787 Adm.Ann Tull late
    Ann Merrill.
MERRILL,Joseph 20 Mar 1784 bonds by
    Elizabeth Merrill exec.,Samuel Tarr, Joshua Guttsore
    Inventory-Elizabeth Merrill exec., next of kin, Sarah
    Tarr,Levi Merrill
MERRILL,Josiah 11 Jun 1784 bonds by
    Ann Merrill adm.,Thomas Merrill, John Mills
    Inventory-Ann Merrill admx. next of kin Thomas Merrill,
    William Smith

15

MERRILL, Elizabeth 21 Dec 1784 bonds by
    (Jacob Boston and Sarah Boston renounce administration
    of Mr.(Joseph) and Mrs. Merrills estate)
    Ann Merrill exec.,John Bishop adm.,William Bishop,
    James Stevenson
    Inventory- Ann Merrill, John Bishop execs. next of
    kin-Levi Henderson, Sarah Boston

MERRILL, William 3 Dec 1783 Inventory
    John Martin adminstrator

MERRILL, Jacob 6 Jul 1787 bonds by
    Samuel Adams Harper,Joshua Duer,Levin Reed

MIDGLEY, Margaret 11 Dec 1788 bonds by
    Thomas Purnell of Wallops Neck,Reuben Cropper, Nathaniel
    Cropper

MIDGELY, Thomas 15 May 1776 inventory
    Thomas Purnell adm., next of kin, Thomas Smith, Isaac Taylo

MILLER, Nathaniel 9 Feb 1784 inventory
    Came Duncan Murray who married the extx. of Nathaniel

MILLS, William 26 Mar 1784 bonds by
    Susanna Burton H.Mills admx.,George Lowe, Joseph Riggs
    Inventory-Susanna Mills adm. next of kin, Richard Mills
    and Jonathan Poarsons

MILLS, Robert 2 Jun 1784 Elizabeth Mills exec. bonds by
    John Mills, Jonathan Stevenson
    Inventory-Elizabeth Mills. next of kin Hugh Mills,
    and John Mills

MILLS, William 19 Dec 1786 bonds by
    William Mills exec.,Samuel McMaster,Elijah Burnett
    Inventory-Wm.Mills exec.,next of kin, Hugh Mills, Tabitha
    Smith

MORE, Hannah 20 Jun 1779 inventory
    Nathan Milbourn exec., next of kin, James Benson,
    Sally Milbourn, Sally Milbourn

MORRIS, Justice 15 Jan 1787 bonds by
    Rachel Morris admx., John Postly,Belitha Powell
    Inventory-Rachel Morris adm., next of kin, Samuel R.
    Morris, Molly Round

MORRIS, Isaac 25 Jan 1783 bonds by
    Sarah Morris adm.,Whitta Bowen adm.,Josiah Mitchell
    Whittington Bowen
    Inventory-Whittington Bowen exec. next of kin,William
    Bowen and Whitt^n Bowen

MORRIS, John 15 Mar 1783 inventory
    Adm. James Round Morris next of kin, William M$_o$rris,
    Justus Morris

MORRIS, Joshua 5 Aug 1782 inventory
    next of kin-John Benson, Jamima Morris
    19 Aug 1784 came Tabitha Stevenson late Tabitha Morris admx

MUMFORD,Charles 31 Aug 1785 bonds by
    Margaret Mumford exec.,John Dennis, Zadock Powell
    inventory-Margaret Cordrey late Margaret Mumford exec.
    29 Aug 1786 next of kin-Elisha Mumford,Jemima Godfrey

MUMFORD,James 2 May 1788 bonds by
    Shadrack Mumford, Elijah Laws Sr.Thomas Cottingham

MUMFORD,James 10 Dec 1788 bonds by
    James Mumford,Sarah Mumford,Robert Schoolfield, Laban Johnson
    Inventory- James Mumford Fassitt exec. next of kin,
    John Fassitt, James Mumford

MUMFORD,Nicholas 12 Dec 1783 bonds
    George Martin adm.,James Martin,Robert M.Richardson
    Inventory-George Martin adm., next of kin, Nancy Mumford
    and Sally Mumford

MUMFORD,Thomas 2 Feb 1788 bonds by
    (Eleanor Mumford w/o Thomas rejects to Joshua Townsend)
    Joshua Townsend Esq. adm.,Solomon Bradford,Henry Parker
    Inventory-Joshua Townsend adm. next of kin Charles Mumford
    and James Mumford

MURRAY,Isaac 4 Jun 1785 inventory
    Margarrt Fassitt exec. next of kin, Isaac Purnell,
    Duncan Murray, John T.Mitchell

MURRAY,William 27 Jun 1789 bonds by
    Margaret Fassitt admx.,Robert Mitchell,Joshua Mitchell
    Inventory-Margaret Fassitt admx. next of kin, Margaret
    Murray and Mary Murray

McFADDEN,Daniel 26 Oct 1787 bonds by
    William Christie adm.,Edward Hammond,James Givan
    Inventory-William Christie adm. no kin as deceased
    was lately from Ireland

NEWBOLD,Smart 12 Apr 1785 bonds by
    Esther Newbold adm.,Isaac Ayres,William Franklin of Edward
    Inventory-Esther Newbold adm. next of kin,Elijah Brittingham

NELSON,Jonathan 20 Feb 1784 bonds by
    (Mary Bell Nelson wid/o Jonathan renounces adm.)
    John Outten Sturgis adm.,James Stevenson,Hugh Stevenson
    Inventory-John Outten Sturgis adm. next of kin,Hugh
    Nelson,Jessee Nelson

NEWTON,Eleanor 19 Dec 1788 bonds by
    (William Allen adm. of Nelly Newton rejects adm.)
    Inventory-(name here is spelled NEWLAND) Dr.Moses Allen
    adm.next of kin-William Allen, Peter Chaille

NICHOLSON,John 14 Nov 1788 bonds by
    Joseph Nicholson,William Dicerson, Barkley White
    Inventory-Joseph Nicholson adm., next of kin,Isaac Nicholson

ORRS,John 31 Mar 1781 Inventory
    Matthew Steel adm. no kin listed

OTTWELL, James 18 May 1787 Bonds by
    Tabitha Ottwell exec., William Ottwell
    Inventory-Tabitha Otwell exec., next of kin Absalom
    Townsend and Epherim Townsend

OUTTEN, John 13 May 1785 bonds by
    Martha Outten adm., Benjamin Davis, William Burbage
    Inventory-Martha Outten admx., next of kin, Comfort
    Outten and Elizabeth Outten

OUTTEN, Comfort 10 Feb 1789 bonds by
    Elizabeth Outten exec., Levi Jones, William Truitt
    Inventory-Elizabeth Outten exec., next of kin, James
    Godfrey, Samuel Johnson

PARKER, Charles 16 Feb 1788 bonds by
    Selby Parker adm., Schoolfield Parker, John Selby of Ezekiel
    Inventory-Selby Parker adm. next of kin, John Parker,
    Ann Parker

PARKER, Elisha 7 Dec 1787 bonds by
    John Parker exec. Elisha Parker exec. Samuel Hearn,
    William Morris s/o Thomas
    Inventory-John and Elisha Parker execs. next of kin,
    Jacob Parker and George Parker

PARKER, Scarbrough 11 Apr 1788 bonds by
    Mary Parker exec., Samuel Taylor, James Selby of Ezekiel
    Inventory-Mary Parker exec., next of kin, Schoolfield
    Parker and William Parker

PARKER, Sacker 6 Jul 1783 bonds by
    Ann Parker exec., Levin Davis Scarborough Parker
    Inventory-Annn Parker exec. signed by William Parker
    Scarborough Parker, Selby Parker

PARKER, Tabitha 1 May 1776 Inventory
    Scarborough Parker Adm. 11 Aug 1786 next of kin, Selby
    Parker and Henry Parker Jr.

PARKER, William Anderson 28 Nov 1788 bonds by
    Rebecca Parker exec., Joshua Townsend, John Wright
    Inventory-Rebecca Parker exec. next of kin, Henry Parker
    and William Parker

PARREMORE, John 27 Jul 1787 bonds by
    Mary Parramore exec., George Martin of Thomas, Robert
    Richardson
    Inventory-Mary Parramore exec., next of kin-William
    Parramore Sr. and William Parramore Jr.

PATTERSON, James 11 Jan 1788 bonds by
    Sarah Patterson exec., Anderson Patterson exec. Isaac
    Boston, John Miller
    Inventory-Sarah and Anderson Patterson execs., next of
    Kin, Bridget Patterson, Revel Patterson

PATTEY, James 13 May 1783 bonds by
    Powell Pattey adm., Robert Dennis, James Givans

PATTEY, John 11 Dec 1785 bonds by
    (unadministered by Powell Pattey former adm.)
    Rachel Pattey adm., Samuel Truitt, Powell Pattey

PATTEY, Powell 11 Dec 1785 bonds by
    Rachel Pattey admx., Samuel Truitt, Powell Pattey
    Inventory-Rachel Pattey adm., next of kin, Mary
    Truitt and George Truitt

PATTEY, Zeno 14 Dec 1785 bonds by
    Rachel Pattey adm. Samuel Truitt, Powell Pattey
    Inventory-Rachel Pattey adm. next of kin, Annanias
    Hudson, Kendal Pattey

PERKINS, Michael 4 Apr 1785 Additional Inventory
    John Perkins exec., next of kin, Betty Perkins and
    Erasmus Harrison

PERKINS, Thomas 22 Apr 1785 bonds by
    Mary Perkins adm., Powell Pattey, Moses Chaille
    Inventory-Mary Perkins adm. next of kin, Asa Coe,
    Erasmus Harrison

PETTITT, Edward 17 Jan 1783 bonds by
    Esther Pettitt exec. Joshua Selby, Robert Richardson
    Inventory-Esther Pettitt exec. next of kin Absalom
    Pettitt and Ephraim Pettitt

PEWSY, David 20 May 1790 Inventory
    Rachel Pewsy exec. next of kin, George Pewsy, Levi
    Lankford

POLLITT, Nehemiah 15 Apr 1785 bonds by
    George Pollitt adm., Stephen Toadvine, Charles Roach
    Inventory-George Pollitt adm. next of kin, William
    Toadvine, Jonathan Pollitt

PORTER, John 17 Oct 1783 bonds by
    Comfort Porter admx., Dennis Hudson, Purnell Porter
    Inventory- Comfort Porter admx., next of kin, Purnell
    Porter and Samuel Porter

POWELL, Mordicai 10 Apr 1786 bonds by
    (we give adm. to Abijah Davis, Thomas Powell Sr.
    Zadock Powell Sr. Thomas Powell s/o Thomas, Annanias
    Powell, Jessee Powell)
    Abijah Davis adm. Zadock Powell, John Powell
    Inventory-Abijah Davis adm. next of kin, John Powell
    and Annanias Powell

PRICE, Rebecca 14 Mar 1788 bonds by
    Arthur Price exec., Hezekiah Johnson, Nehemiah Dorman
    Inventory-Arthur Price exec. next of kin, Nathaniel
    Davis, John Conner

POWELL, John 15 Feb 1783 inventory
    Adenah Powell exec. next of kin, Jessee Powell, Thomas Powell

PRICE, William 26 Sep 1783 bonds by
    Rebecca Price adm. Eliakim Johnson, Nathaniel Davis
    Inventory-Rebecca Price exec. next of kin-Arter Price
    and Betty Price

PROBART, Yelverton 7 Dec 1786 bonds by
    (Leah Probart rejects adm. of husbands est. who died
    intestate to friends Uncle William Lane and John
    Done to adm.
    4 May 1787 Dohn Done, Thomas Martin of James and James
    Round Morris (Inventory of estate in hands of Leah
    Probart now in Jones County N.C.)

PURNELL, Mary 15 Jun 1787 bonds by
    John Fassitt Jr., Thomas Purnell Esq.(Sinepuxent),
    Reuben Cropper
    Inventory-John Fassitt exec., next of kin, Thomas S.
    Fassitt and John Marshall

PURNELL, Thomas of Thomas 9 Mar 1784 bonds by
    James Purnell adm., Benjamin Purnell, Thomas Purnell
    (of Wallops Neck.)
    Inventory-Adm. James Purnell, next of kin, Zadock Marshall
    and Isaac Purnell

PURNELL, Peter 15 Dec 1789 bonds by
    Catherine Purnell exec., Isaac Marshall esq. Matthew Purnell
    Inventory-Catherine Purnell ex. next of kin Isaac Purnell
    and Matthew Purnell

PURNELL, John 15 Jan 1789 bonds by
    Elizabeth Purnell exec, Robert Purnell exec., John Selby
    Outten Sturgis esq.
    Inventory of John Purnell of John- Betsy & Robert Purnell ex
    next of kin, Mary Wright, Joshua Sturgis

PURNELL, Matthew 3 Apr 1787 bonds by
    Elizabeth Purnell exec., Joshua Hodge, Rives Rackliffe
    Inventory-Elizabeth Purnell admx., next of kin, Elisha
    Purnell and Benjamin Purnell

PURNELL, Matthew 30 May 1786 bonds by
    Elizabeth Purnell exec, Isaac Ayres, Elisha Purnell

PURNELL Matthew 8 Sep 1787 bonds by
    (unadministered by Elizabeth Purnell since deceased.)
    Isaac Ayres adm.m James Fassitt, Peter Parker

PURNELL, Lambert 25 Jan 1783 bonds by
    Annanias Hudson, Samuel Hopkins, James H. Round
    Inventory- Isaac Ayres adm. next of kin Elisha Purnell
    and Matthew Purnell

PURNELL, Elizabeth 8 Sep 1787 bonds by
    Isaac Ayres, James Fassitt, Peter Parker

PURNELL, Levi 30 Dec 1789 bonds by
    Delilah Purnell adm., Elisha Purnell, Joshua Townsend

PURNELL, Walton, 29 Oct 1787 bonds by
    Catherine Purnell, Benjamin Purnell, Isaac Purnell, John Pope

PURNELL, William 25 Aug 1783 inventory
    Mary Elizabeth Purnell exec., next of kin, Zadock Purnell
    and Thomas Purnell

PURNELL, William 8 Apr 1785 Inventory
    Mary Purnell & Isaac Houston execs.(Inventory on Croppers
    Island, on Hudsons Neck, on Phoenixes Island) next of
    kin-Benjamin Purnell, Matthew Purnell

QUINTON, Dixon 26 Aug 1783 bonds by
    Phillip Quinton adm., William Merrill, James Quinton
    Inventory-Phillip Quinton adm., next of kin, Jacob
    Adams, Abegal Collins

QUINTON, Tabitha 17 Nov 1784 bonds by
    James Quinton, William Merrill, Elijah Boston
    Inventory-James Quinton exec., next of kin, Phillip
    Quinton, Mary Dixon

RACKLIFFE, Charles 9 Mar 1784 bonds by
    Charles Rackliff, James Wilson Peter Chaille
    Inventory- Charles Rackliffe exec. next of kin John
    Rackliffe and Nathaniel Rackliffe

RACKLIFFE, Charles 7 Apr 1787 bonds by
    William Stevenson, Charles Taylor, Levi Mills

    Inventory William Stevenson exec., next of kin, Zadock
    Purnell and Thomas Purnell

RACKLIFFE, Nathaniel 11 Dec 1789 bonds by
    Mary Rackliffe exec., James Fassitt, Charles Rackliffe
    Inventory-Mary Rackliffe exec., next of kin, John Rackliffe
    and Charles Rackliffe

RACKLIFFE, John 13 Jan 1787 bonds by
    (Thomas Purnell and Charles Rackliffe rejects adm.)
    James Rackliffe exec, Hampton Rounds exec., Charles Rackliffe
    Inventory- next of kin, James Rackliffe and Charles Rackliffe

RACKLIFFE, Thomas 4 Sep 1789 bonds by
    John W. Rounds, James R. Morris, Thomas Martin

RAMSEY, Sarah 30 Jul 1785 bonds by
    John Miller exec., Levi Mills esec. Agnes Mills exec, Isaac
    Evans and William Undrill
    Inventory-John Miller exec., next of kin, John Kerby
    and Isabella Miller

RAIN(Rane)Phillip 4 Feb 1786 bonds by
    Henry Parker adm., Selby Parker, Joseph Kellam
    Inventory-Henry Parker adm. next of kin, John Rain and
    Martha Rain

REED, Littleton 20 Nov 1784 bonds by
    Mary Reed admx., Solomon Carey, John Tarr
    Inventory- Mary Read ex., next of kin, John Read and Major
    Read

REED, Pierce 23 Jan 1784 bonds by
    (Seaiahr Reed widow renounces admin.)
    John Read adm., Levi Beachboard, James Lindsay
    Inventory- John Reed adm. next of kin, James Reed, Levin Reed

RICHARDSON, Robert 18 Jan 1788 bonds by
    John Bishop adm., Benjamin Bishop, Major Townsend
    Inventory-John Bishop adm. next of kin, Levi Richardson
    and Robert Richardson

RICHARDSON, William 9 Sep 1785
    (Nancy Richardson rejects adm. of father Wm.'s est.)
    Robert Martin Richardson adm., Jessee Bennett, William
    Stevens Hill
    Inventory of Capt. William- Robert Martin Richardson adm.
    Next of kin-Polly Smith and Nancy Selby 28 Jan 1786

RIGGIN, Darby 13 Feb 1789 bonds by
    Hannah Riggin exec., Robert Richardson, Jr., Levin Riggin
    Inventory-Hannah Riggin exec., next of kin, Comfort
    Atkinson and Grace Riggin

RIGGIN, Jonathan 7 Sep 1784 bonds by
    Jessee Fooks exec., Alexander Porter, Moses Lank
    Ineventory, Jessee Fooks exec., next of kin, Elaner
    Causey, Nancy Riggin

Roach, James, Sarah Roach adm., John Cathell, David Cathell
    15 Mar 1785 bonds
    Inventory, Sarah Roach adm., next of kin, Levin Roach,
    Charles Roach

ROACH, Mary 11 Apr 1785 bonds by
    (Sarah Cannon rejects adm.)
    Leah Glass adm, Christopher Glass, Zadock Sturgis
    Inventory(debts due) 12 Jul 1789 Leah Winbrow late
    Leah Glass adm. no kin listed

ROBINS, Bowdoin 12 Nov 1784 bonds by
    Daniel Robins exec., William Handy exec., Henry Parker
    Inventory-Daniel Robins & Wm. Handy execs., next of
    kin-Littleton Robins, Mary Purnell

ROBINS, Bowdoin 25 Feb 1787 bonds by
    Littleton Robins, Nathaniel Ennis, William Parker

ROBINS, Josiah, 15 Mar 1785 bonds by
    Joshua Townsend, Mary Robins adm., John Wright
    Inventory-Mary Robins adm., next of kin Joseph Tilghman,
    Levi Robins

ROBINS, Thomas 20 Feb 1787 bonds by
    Littleton Robins, Nathaniel Ennis, William Parker
    (Unadministered by Arlanta Robins and John Purnell
    Robins both dec'd)
    Inventory- Littleton Robins exec., next of kin, Mary
    Purnell and Esther Robins

ROSSE, John 16 Mar 1776 Reverend, bonds by
    Elizabeth Ross exec. 6 Aug 1784 next of kin;none in county

ROUND, Naomi, 10 Feb 1786 bonds by
    Samuel Hopkins Round, Solomon Long, Edward Vandome

RUARK, James 11 Feb 1786 bonds by
    Esau Williams, Shadrack Ruark adm., Wm. Franklin of Edward
    Inventory- Shadrack Ruark adm. next of kin, Elizabeth
    Downs, William Jackson

SCOTT, Joseph 28 Jan 1785 addl. Inventory
    John Ennals Scott exec., next of kin, Sarah Scott, Sarah
    Atkinson

SELBY, Daniel 27 Aug 1785 bonds by
    Zadock Selby adm., Benjamin McCormack, Nehemiah Latchum
    Inventory-Zadock Selby adm. next of kin, Parker Selby
    and William Selby

SELBY, David 1 Oct 1788 bonds by
    Tabitha Selby admx., Phillip Quinton, John Johnson
    inventory- Tabitha Selby adm., next of kin, Parker
    Selby and John Selby

SELBY, John 7 Jan 1783 bonds by
    Sarah Selby adm., Phillip Selby adm., Michael Tarr,
    Selby Newtown
    Inventory- Sarah and Phillip Selby adms., next of kin,
    Lemuel Johnson, Parker Selby Sr.
    Additional Inv.,-came Phillip Selby adm. and Joseph
    Delastatius who married Sarah Selby Admx.

SELBY, Jessee 5 Dec 1788 bonds by
    Eleanor Selby adm., William Bowin, Parker Selby of Wm.
    Inventory-Eleanor Selby adm., next of kin, Parker
    Selby and Sarah Hudson

SELBY, Capt. John of John 8 Nov 1780 Inventory
    Kendal Smock and Leah his wife adm., next of kin
    James Selby and Parker Selby

SELBY, Mary 16 Feb 1788 Inventory
    signed by Zadock, Selby, John Selby, James Selby,
    Leah Selby adm. of John Selby

SELBY, Phillip 13 Jun 1786 bonds by
    William Holland exec., Lucretia Brumbly, James Linsey
    Inventory-William Holland exec. next of kin, William
    Walton, Parker Selby

SELBY, Parker 3 Dec 1784 bonds by
    Mary Selby adm., John Selby, Zadock Selby
    Inventory- Mary Selby adm., next of kin, Phillip Selby
    and William Walton

SELBY, Parker 1 May 1784 bonds by
    (Mary Selby adm. of estate is also now deceased, rights
    of adm. belongs to me, signed Parker Selby; I renounce.)
    Fisher Walton adm., Kendal Smock adm., Nehemiah Dorman,
    Yelverton P. Probart

SELBY, Parker 8 April 1789 bonds by
    Nancy Selby admx., John Selby, John Selby of Parker

SELBY, Parker (Capt.) 1790 debts of-
    Fisher Walton acting administrator

SELBY, William 23 Nov 1784 bonds by
    Sarah Selby adm., Parker Selby, Jessee Bowen
    Inventory-Sarah Selby exec. next of kin, Parker Selby
    and Parker Selby son of William

SHOCKLEY, Sampson 5 Mar 1783 bonds by
    Betty Shockley adm., Benjamin Shockley, William Morris
    Inventory- Betty Shcokley adm., next of kin, Benjamin
    Shockley and Noble Shockley

SHOCKLEY, Jonathan 25 Jul 1784 bonds by
    Elizabeth Shockley admx., John Cathell, James Roach
    Inventory-Elizabeth Shockley admx., next of kin, Richard
    Trader, Jessee Pokes??

SHOWELL,Samuel 18 Jan 1787 bonds by
    Sarah Showell, Belitha Powell, Erasmus Harrison
    Inventory- no adm.shown. nest of kin, Samuel Showell
    and Betty Holloway

SMITH,Benjamin 10 Aug 1787 bonds by
    Elizabeth Smith adm., Levin Smith, Henry Kelly
    Inventory- Elizabeth Smith adm., next of kin, Elijah
    Smith and Leaven Smith
    8 Aug 1789- came Henry Smith and Elizabeth Smith adminx.

SMITH,George 29 Jan 1788 bonds by
    (George Smith Sr. exec. of George Smith rejects adm.)
    Isaac Cooper exec.,Joshua Townsend,William Selby of SnowHill.
    Inventory-Isaac Cooper exec., next of kin, George Smith
    of Andrs., Marshall Smith (Porder)

SMITH,John O. Norton Smith 28 Jul 1787 bonds by
    Elizabeth Smith exec., Charles Taylor,William Hayward
    Inventory-Elizabeth Smith exec. next of kin,William
    Smith and George McGee

SMITH,John O. Norton and Elizabeth 18 Sep 1789 bonds by
    Charles Taylor,William Hayward, Levin Martin

SMITH,John 22 Nov 1782 Inventory
    Thomas Purnell exec., next of kin, Eleanor Selby,
    Elishal Morris

SMITH,James 12 Jul 1782 Inventory
    by James Selby and Elisha Jones, next of kin, Samuel Smith

SMITH,Samuel 28 Jan 1783 Inventory
    Betty Smith adm., next of kin, John Smith,Samuel Davis

SMOCK,Powell 28 Jul 1787 bonds by
    Elizabeth Smock adm.,William Stevenson,John Rackliffe
    Inventory-Elizabeth Smock admx., next of kin, Holland
    Smock and Jessee Smock

SNEAD,John 31 May 1788 Inventory
    John Selby Esq. adm. no kin known

SPENCE,Adam 23 May 1788 bonds by
    Nancy Spence adm., Capt.Charles Bennitt, John Martin
    Inventory-Nancy Spence adm. next of kin, George Spence
    and Mag^t. Spence

SPENCE,John 20 Nov 1787 bonds by
    Nancy Spence adm. George Martin,Charles Bennett
    Inventory-Nancy Spence adm. next of kin-George Spence
    and Mag. Spence

STEVENS, John 11 Feb 1786 bonds by
    Sophia Stevens adm.,Joshua Stevens adm., Kendall Kennett
    John Walter
    Inventory-Sophia and Joshua Stevens adms. next of kin,
    John Farewell and Joseph ??

STEVENS,William Davis 5 Nov 1777 Inventory
    Sophia Stevens exec. 2 Mar.1783 next of kin, John Farwell
    and Benjamin McCormick

STEVENSON, John 29 Jan 1777 inventory
John Riggin and Sarah his wife admx, 10 Nov 1786
next of kin, Rebecca Stevenson, John Stevenson

STEVENSON, James 8 Jul 1785 bonds by
Rebecca Stevenson exec,, Edward Hammond, Zadock Sturgis
Inventory 23 Jul 1786, Edward Bishop and Rebecca his
wife admx., next of kin, Esther Stevenson, Zadock Stevenson

STEWART, John 25 Aug 1783 bonds by
Mary Stewart adm. Andrew Steward adm., Ebenezer Holloway,
Joseph Gray
Inventory-Mary Stewart exec. Andrew Stewart exec.
next of kin-William Selby and G. Stewart

STOCKLEY, Sophia 25 Oct 1785 bonds by
(unadministered by James Houston dec'd)
William Bell, John Postly, Mathias Hopkins

STOCKLEY, Sophia 18 Feb 1787 bonds by
Levin Bell, William Spiers, Nehemiah Dorman
(unadministered by James Houston dec'd)

STURGIS, William 24 Oct 1783 bonds by
James Guthrey adm., Parker Selby, Joshua Guthrey
Inventory-James Guthrey adm. next of kin, Stephen Sturgis
and Stephen Sturgis

STURGIS, Thomas 19 Nov 1783 bonds
Outten Sturgis adm., Stephen Sturgis, Richard Sturgis
Inventory-Outten Sturgis adm. next of kin, Jonathan
Hutcheson, Elijah Sturgis

STURGIS, Diana 8 Mar 1784 bonds by
Robert Gibbs adm., Nehemiah Dorman, Valentine Dennis
Inventory-Robert Gibbs exec. next of kin Elisha Johnson,
Susan Johnson

STURGIS, William 27 Feb 1784 bonds by
Elijah Sturgis, John Tarr, John Evans

STURGIS, Thomas Purnell 27 Feb 1782 inventory
Zadock Selby exec., next of kin, Outten Sturgis, Mary Selby

TARR, Elisha 2 Jan 1784 bonds by
Esther Tarr adm., Elijah Sturgis, John Tarr of Michael
Inventory-Esther Tarr adm. next of kin, Samuel Tarr,
and John Tarr

TARR, John 28 Jan 1785 Bonds by
Sarah Tarr exec., Isaac Tarr, Samuel Tarr, Outten Sturgis
Inventory-Sarah Tarr exec. next of kin, Samuel Tarr and
Israel Tarr

TARR, Elisha 7 Jun 1785 bonds by
(unadministered by Esther Tarr now dec'd)
John Tarr of Michael, William Campbell, William Tarr

TAYLOR, Alexander 27 May 1788 bonds by
Honor Taylor execx, James Fassitt, James Givan
Inventory-Honor Taylor admx., next of kin, Ezekiel
Taylor and Joshway Taylor

TAYLOR,Alexander 12 Jun 1789 bonds by
    Rachel Taylor, William Kennett, Abijah Davis

TEAGUE,Mary 2 Jan 1787 bonds by
    (George Teague rejects adm. to brother Jacob.)
    Jacob Teague adm.,Patrick Waters,Zadock Sturgis
    Inventory-Jacob Teague adm., next of kin, Nathaniel
    Bratten, George Teague

THOMPSON,James 26 Mar 1783 bonds by
    Sarah Thompson adm., Paul Davis,Levin Carey
    Inventory-Leah Thompson exec. next of kin, Jonathan
    Cathell, Daniel Cathell

THOMPSON,Robert 1 Jan 1889 bonds by
    Thomas Gordon adm.,Jessee Jones,William Undrill
    Inventory-Thomas Gordon adm., no kin known

TIGNAL, Southy 12 Oct 1784 bonds by
    Tabitha Tignal admx.,John Harrison, Reuben Magee
    Inventory-Tabitha Tignal admx. next of kin, John
    Harrison and William Vines

TILLETT,Thomas 11 Feb 1786 bonds by
    Tabitha Tillett,admx.,Josiah Mitchell, Kendall Kennett
    Inventory-Admx.Tabitha Tillett, no kin in state

TOADVINE,Ezekiel 11 Dec 1784 bonds by
    Levin Carey adm.,Thomas Fooks, John Twonsend

TOADVINE,Purnell 29 Jul 1783 bonds by
    William Toadvine adm.,Levi Outten,John Townsend
    Inventory-Wm.Toadvine adm., next of kin, John Toadvine,
    Henry Toadvine

TOWNSEND,Brickhouse 23 Oct 1789 Inventory
    Jeremiah Townsend exec., next of kin, William Townsend
    and Luke Townsend

TOWNSEND,Bartly 8 Jun 1782 Inventory
    Jemimia Townsend exec. next of kin-William Selby(S.H.)
    and William Selby Sr.

TOWNSEND,Danford 16 Mar 1784 bonds by
    Epharim Townsend adm.,Absalom Townsend,Joshua Townsend
    Inventory-Ephraim Townsend exec., next of kin, James
    Townsend and Absalom Townsend

TOWNSEND,Jeremiah 17 Feb 1784 bonds by
    Joshua Townsend Esq.adm.,Major Townsend adm., Nehemiah
    Dorman, Nathaniel Bratten
    Inventory-Joshua and Major Townsend adms. next of kin
    Bartley Townsend and John Bell

TOWNSEND,James 9 Dec 1783 bonds by
    Sarah Townsend admx.,James Williams, Thomas Barnes,
    Jonathan Hudson
    Inventory- Sarah Townsend adm., next of kin, Esther
    Quinton and Phillip Quinton

TOWNSEND,Luke 7 Apr 1789 bonds by
    Isaac Cottingham exec. Experience Cottingham, Francis
    Randall, James Duer
    Inventory of Luke Townsend late of New York City- Isaac
    Cottingham exec. next of kin, Eleanor Stevans, Levi
    Townsend

TRUITT, Henry 13 Jun 1783 bonds by
William Truitt adm., Thomas Cottingham, William Truitt Sr.
Inventory-Wm. Truitt adm. next of kin Rownd Truitt and
Edward Truitt

TRUITT, Job 6 May 1785 bonds by
George Truitt, exec., William Jarman Bethards exec. John
Parsons, James Jarman
Inventory-George Truitt exec. William Jarman Bethards exec.,
next of kin-George and Outten Truitt

TRUITT, Pattey 13 Apr 1781 Inventory
Whittington Bowen and Rachel his wife exec. 15 Feb 1783
next of kin, Kendal Pattey, Powell Patey

TRUITT, William 24 Apr 1787 Inventory
Ann Downs late Ann Truitt, w/o James Downs, execx.
next of kin, Littleton Truitt and Jarman Truitt

TURNER, Theopilus 5 Jul 1785 bonds by
(Unise Turner gives adm. to son Jackson Turner)
Jackson Turner adm., Thomas Cottingham, Barkley White
Inventory-Jackson Turner adm., next of kin, George
Turner and Elizabeth Hudson

WALTER, John 26 Oct 1784 bonds by
Solomon Walter, Dennis Hudson, Elias Pennewell

WALTER, John 3 May 1788 bonds by
Comfort Walter exec., Zeno Evans, John Lindall
Inventory-Comfort Walter exec. next of kin, Anny
Showell, Zeno Evans

WARD, James 19 Mar 1784 Bonds by
Priscilla Ward adm., John Shockley, Richard Shockley
Inventory-Priscilla Ward exec., no kin listed

WARREN, Pharoch 8 Nov 1788 bonds by
Elizabeth Warren exec., Levi Mills, William Stevenson
Inventory-Elizabeth Warren exec., next of kin, Thomas
Warren, John Warren

WATTS, Charles 28 Jan 1786 bonds by
Rachel Ayres adm., John Johnson, John Ayres
Inventory-Rachel Ayres adm., next of kin, Martha March,
John Selby

WHALEY, Elias 21 Feb 1776 Inventory
Martha Bishop late Martha Whaley exec. 29 Jun 1789
next of kin, Seth Whaley and Esther Whaley

WHITE, Barkley 4 Mar 1789 bonds by
Margaret White adm., Thomas Selby, William Jones
Inventory-Margaret White adm. next of kin, Major White
and Joshua White

WHITE, Henry 30 Aug 1785 bonds by
Mary White adm., Joshua Hodge, Whittington Bowen
Inventory-Mary White adm. next of kin John White, Stephen
White (8 Sep 1786 came Joseph Green and Mary his wife adminx.)

WHITE, John 16 Oct 1784 bonds by
   (Major White brother of dec'd renounces admin.)
   John Ball adm., John Townsend, William White
   Inventory-John Ball adm., next of kin, William White
   and Major White

WHITE, William 26 Feb 1785 bonds by
   Ann Hickman adm. Josiah Mitchell, John Pope
   Inventory-26 Jul 1788 Ann Holloway late Ann Hickman admx.
   next of kin, Mary White and Ann Hickman

WHITTINGTON, Southy 27 Dec 1786 bonds by
   Southy Whittington ex., Col. Samuel Handy, David Long
   Inventory-Southy Whittington exec. next of kin, Aaron
   Sterling and J. Gunby

WILLIAMS, John 26 Nov 1783 Inventory
   Nanney Williams adm. next of kin, Joseph Stevenson,
   Betty Williams

WILLIS, John 7 Apr 1787 bonds by
   Tabitha Willis exec., Levi Mills, Lemuel Franklin
   Inventory-Tabitha Willis exec.
   signed by, William Jackson, David Willis, Margaret Fassitt,
   Joseph Green exec. of Henry White

WISE, William 30 Jan 1786 bonds by
   (Sarah Wise relinquishes adm. of dec'd husbands est.)
   James Martin Adm., Thomas Martin, James Round Morris
   Inventory-James Martin adm., next of kin, Matthew
   Hopkins and Samuel Hopkins

WISE, Samuel Capt. 2 Feb 1787 bonds by
   (Sarah Wise rejects adm.)
   George Martin of Thomas adm., George Purnell, Robert
   Martin Richardson
   Inventory-George Martin adm. next of kin, John Wise
   and John M. Wise

WOOLSEY, Daniel 1 Nov 1782 Inventory
   Col. Samuel Handy adm. no kin known in state

WRIGHT, Zadock 4 Sep 1789 bonds by
   Mary Wright, Thomas Martin, James Round

WYATT, Caleb 3 Oct 1785 bonds by
   Sarah Wyatt exec., Samuel Bratten, Samuel Richardson
   inventory-Sarah Wyatt exec., next of kin, Anny Wyatt,
   Rhoday Murray

YOUNG, Milby 8 Mar 1786 bonds by
   Mary Young adm., Daniel Young, John Houston
   Inventory- Mary Young adm. next of kin, Ezekiel Young
   and Daniel Young

End of Book

Administrators & Kin Index

ADAMS,Jacob-21
ALLEN-Moses-17
  Wm.-7-17
ATKINSON-James-14
  Comfort-22
  Sarah-22
AYRES-Henry-5
  Isaac-2-10-13
    17-20
  John-11-12-27
  Rachel-27
BAIN-Stephen-10
BAINUM-Wm.-9
  John-28
BAKER-Wm.-8
  Solomon-8
BARNS-Thomas-7-26
BEACHBOARD-Levi-21
BELL-Levin-25
  John-26
  William-25
BENNETT-Wm.-11-12
  Charles-11-24
  Jessee-6-10-21
BENSON-Elias-8
  James-16
  John-16
  Josiah-14
  Robert-14
  Nehemiah-2
BETHARDS,Wm.-27
BEVANS-Wm.-3
BIGLAND-Wm.-6
BISHOP-Edward-25
  Benjamin-21
  Elizabeth-10
  Elizabeth-10
  John-9-15-16-21
  Martha-27
  William-16
BLADES-Ballard-2
BLAKE-Levin-1
BOND-Rhoda-11
BOSTON-Isaac-4-18
  Elijah-21
  Jacob-16
  Sarah-15-16
BOWEN-Jessee-23
  Rachel-27
  Whittha-16
  Whittington-14-
    16-27
BRADFORD-Annanais-13
  Solomon-17
BRATTEN-Samuel-28
  Nathaniel-10-26
BRAVARD-John-13

BRUINGTON-James-2
  John-7
BRITTINGHAM-Mary-11
  Belitha-6
  Elijah-17
  Purnell-13
BURBAGE-Wm-18
BRUMBLY-Lucretia-23
BURNETT-Elijah-16
CAMPBELL-Wm.-25
CANNON-Sarah-22
CAREY-Levin-9-26
  Samuel-11
  Solomon-21
BATHELL-Levi-12
  David-22
  Daniel-26
  John-7-22-23
  Jonathan-26
CAUSEY-Eleanor-22
CHAILLE-Peter-1-2-
  6-8-20-21
  Moses-11-13-19
CHRISTIE-Wm.-17
CHRISTOPHER
  Stephen-5
  Elizabeth-10
COE-Asa-19
COLLINS-Abigail-21
COLLYER-Peter-9
CONNER-John-19
  Levinah-3
COOPER-Isaac-24
CORBIN-Wm.,-3
CORDREY-Margaret-17
COTTINGHAM-Isaac-26
  Experience-26
  Daniel-8
  Thomas-4-17-27
CROPPER-Edmund-12
  Reuben-14-16-20
  Nathaniel-16
CURLIS-Elizabeth-14
DALE-Thomas-2-8-10
DAVIS-Abisha-12
  Abijah-19-20
  Benjamin-18
  Jessee-8
  Levin-18
  Matthew-4
  Micajah-10
  Nathaniel-4-19
  Paul-26
  Samuel-10-24
  Spencer-3
  William-9
DELASTATIUS-
  Joseph-23

DENNIS-Atkins-1
  Ann-1
  Benjamin-1
  John-12-17
  Robert-18
DICKESON-DICKERSON
  Josiah-5
  Eleanor-9
  William-17
Dixon-Mary-21
DONE-John-6-8-20
DORMAN-Nehemiah-10-
  12-14-19-23-25-26
DOWNEY-Somerset-5
DOWNS-Ann-27
  Elizabeth-22
DRYDEN-John-14
  William-4
DUER-James-4-26
  Joshua-16
DUNCAN-Isaac
EARGER-William-14
ENNALS-John-1
ENNIS-Nathaniel-22
EVANS-Isaac-11-21
  John-25
  Joseph-6
  Mary-12
  Zeno-27
FAREWELL-John-24
FASSITT-David-14
  Elijah-15
  James-17-20-21-25
  John-12-15-17-20
  Margaret-6-17-27
  Rouse-6-12-13
  Thomas-20
  William-12-13
FERN-Samuel-10
FLEMING-John-11
FLINT-John-6
FOOKS-Jessee-22
  Thomas-7-26
FRANKLIN-Alexander-12
  Edward-17-22
  Henry-1-11-12-13-15
  Eleanor-12
  Lemuel-1-28
  Peal-15
  William-15-17-22
GIBBS-Robert-25
GIVAN-James-4-17-18-25
GLASS-Leah-22
  Christopher-22
GORDON-Thomas-26
GODFREY-James-10-18
  Jemima-17

GRAY-Jacob-13
  Elizabeth-13
  Joseph-13-25
GREEN-Mary-27-28
  Joseph-4-8-10-27
GUNBY-J-28
GUTHREY-James-25
  Joshua-12-25
GUTTSORE-Joshua-15
HALL-Richard-14
HAMMOND-Elizabeth-6
  Edward-5-6-10-17-25
  Molly D.-8
  William-13
HANDY-Wm.-4-5-8-22
  Samuel-5-7-12-28
HARPER-Samuel-16
HARRISON-John-26
  Erasmus-19-24
HAYWARD-Sarah-2
  William-24
HAZZARD-Christian-2
HEARN-Samuel-18
HENDERSON-Levi-16
  James-3
HENRY-Edward-5
HICKMAN-Ann-28
HILL-Isaac-3-11
  Nancy-11
  Wm.S.-4-11-12-13-21
HODGE-Joshua-9-20-27
HOLLAND-Levi-8
  Benjamin-11
  Wm.,-1-8-23
HOLLOWAY-Betty-24
  Ebenezer-25
  Ann-28
  Jessee-4
HOOK-Mary-5
  William-5
HOPKINS-Levin-14
  Mary-14
  Mathias-25
  Hampton-3-6-13-14
  Matthew-1-2-5-14-28
  Samuel-28
HOUSTON-Levi-2
  Isaac-8-20
  James-25
  John-28
  Francis-7
HUDSON-Eli-5
  Annanias-5-14-19
  Benjamin-3-12
  Dennis-5-19-27
  Elizabeth-27

HUDSON-Laban-1
  Mary-12
  McKimmy-2
  Joseph-15
  Jonathan-26
  Robert-3
  Sarah-23
  Solomon-3
  Thomas-3
HUTCHESON-Jonathan 10-23
INGERSOL-Samuel-9
  Richard-9
INGRAM_Samuel-
JACKSON-Wm.-22-28
JARMAN-Annanias-6
JOHNSON-Elisha-25
  Ezekiah-15
  Eliakim-19
  Hezekiah-19
  John-1-11-23-27
  Laban-17
  Lemuel-23
  Samuel-3-8-18
  Susan-25
JONES-Elisha-24
  Jessee-9-11-26
  John-11-13
  Levi-18
  Thomas-1-13
  William-27
KELLAM_Joseph-21
KELLY-Henry-24
KENNETT-Wm.-26
  Kendal-8-24-26
KERBY-John-3-21
KING-Levy-10
LAMDEN-Mary-11
LANE-Wm.,-20
LANK-Moses-22
LANKFORD-Levi-19
LATCHUM-Nehemiah-8-22
LAYFIELD-John-8
  Thomas-8
LAWS-Isaac-11
  Elijah-11-16
  James-5
  Nancy-11
LEWIS-George-8
LINDALL-John-27
LINDSAY-James-21-23
LIVINGSTON-Sarah-12
  George-12
LOCKWOOD-Samuel-8
LONG-Armwell-12
  David-28
  Littleton-2-7

LONG-Solomon-4-15-22
LOWE-George-16
MADDUX-Hezekiah-9
  Zerababel-1
MAGLAMMRY-Ann-1
MARCH-Martha-27
MARSHALL-Isaac-20
  John-7-20
  Zadock-20
MARTIN-Charlotte-2
  George-1-17-18-24-28
  James-1-5-9-17-20-28
  John-16-24
  Levin-24
  Robert-3
  Thomas-10-18-20-21-28
MELSON-Daniel-9-10
MELVIN-Robert-3
MERRILL-Comfort-5
  Elijah-5
  Joseph-4
  William-2-7-13-14-21
MILBOURN-Elizabeth-14
  Nathan-16
  Sally-16
  William-7
MILLER-Joseph-9
  John-11-18-21
  Isabella-21
MILLS-Agnes-15-21
  John-15
  Levi-8-21-27-28
  Rachel-14
MITCHELL-Joshua-1-17
  Josiah-1-4-5-6-7-11-16-26-28
  John-9-17
  Joseph-14
  Robert-17
MORRIS-Elisha-24
  Cornelius-2
  James R.-1-20-21-28
  Thomas-18
  Sarah-3
  William-7-18-23
MUMFORD-Eleanor-11
  James-10
  Turvill-1
MURRAY-Duncan-16-17

McALLEN-Alexander-2
McCORMACK-Benjamin-6-8-9-14-22-24
McDANIEL-William-8
McGEE-George-24
  Reuben-26
McMASTER-Samuel-16

NEWTON-Selby-1-15-23
NOBLE-William-4

OUTTEN-Levi-26

PARKE-Moses-12
PARKER-Ayres-1
  Charles-2
  George-8
  Henry-11-12-13-
    17-21-22
  James-6-9-13
  John-6-10
  Mary-11
  Peter-13-20
  Rhoda-8
  Schoolfield-11
  Selby-6-13-15-21
  William-1-11-12-
    22
PARSONS-Jonathan-16
PENNEWELL-Elias-27
PERDUE-James-3-15
PERKINS-John-4-13-14
  Solomon-4
PHILLIPS-Isaac-5-14
PITTS-Hillary-3-10-
  13-14
POLK-William-9
POPE-John-20-28
PORTER-Alexander-22
  McKimmy-2-4
  Margaret-13
POSTLY-John-7-12-
  16-25
POWELL-Belitha-7-16-
  24
  Zadock-17
PRIDEAUX-John-8
PORBART-Yelverton-23
PURNELL-Elisha-12
  Benjamin-2-4-6-13
  George-8-28
  Isaac-8-13-17
  James-6
  Levi-13
  Mary-22
  Matthew-12
  Thomas-7-16-20-21-24
  Walton-4-8
  William-1-6-7-8-9-11
  Zadock-21

QUILLEN-Benjamin=8
QUINTON-James-13-21
  Esther-26
  Phillip-14-23-26

RACKLIFFE-Charles-9
  John-24
  Rives-20

RANDAL-Francis-1-26
REED-Levin-16
  Mary-6
RICHARDS-John-9-13
RICHARDSON-John-1
  Joseph-3-8
  Robert-4-10-17-18
    19-22-28
  Samuel-28
RIGGIN-John-25
  Joshua-9
  Sarah-25
RIGGS-Joseph-16
RILEY-Levin-15
ROACH-Charles-19
  James-23
ROAN-Esther-14
ROBINS-Littleton-6
ROBINSON-Levi-4
  Henderson-4
  Josiah-4
ROUND-Hampton-21
  James-28
  John-21
  Samuel-4-9
ROWLEY-Richard-9

SAVAGE-Isaac-2-4
  Mary-2
SCARBOROUGH-John-3
SCHOOLFIELD-Robert-
  6-10-17
SELBY-Eleanor-24
  Ezekiel-18
  Jessee-5-12
  John-2-3-5-10-18
    20-24-27
  James-4-18-24
  Joshua-19
  Mary-25
  Matthew-15
  Nancy-21
  Parker-5-8-15-25
  Phillip-13
  Tabitha-11
  Thomas-9-27
  William-11-14-24-
    25-26
  Zadock-2-3-5-25
SHOCKLEY-Elijah-1-2
  John-27
  Richard-27
SHOWELL-Anny-27
SLATTERY-Bartholomew
  1-13
SLOCOMB-Robert-2
SLOTH-William-4
SMART-Henry-14

SMITH-Levi-13
  Polly-21
  John-16
  Thomas-16
  Walter-14
  William-15
SMOCK-Holland-7
  Kendal-23
  Leah-23
SPENCER-Sarah-10
SPIERS-William-25
STEEL-Matthew-7
STERLINH-Aaron-28
STEVENS-Eleanor-26
  Sophia-8
STEVENSON-Hugh-17
  George-6
  James-2-16-12-17
  Jonathan-2-16
  Joseph-28
  Mary-12
  Tabitha-16
  William-3-4-12-21-
    24-27
STURGIS-Elijah-1-25
  John-10-17
  Joshua-20
  Levin-2
  Outten-5-20-25
  Stephen-5
  Zadock-9-22-25-26
SULLIVAN-William-14

TARR-Michael-23
  Sarah-15
  Samuel-2-15
  John-21-25
TAYLOR,Ezekiel-25
  Charles-8-24-21
  Leah-14
  George-14
  Isaac-16
  John-13-14
  Laban-8
  Samuel-18
TEACKLE-John-7
  Elizabeth-7
TEAGUE-George-4
TILGHMAN-Joseph-7-22
TIMMONS-Elijah-4
TINDALL-John-13
TINGLE-Caleb-6-12-14-15
TOADVINE-Henry-7
  Rhoda T-2
  Stephen-19
  William-19

TOWNSEND-Ann-4
  Absalom-18
  Barkley-2
  Ephraim-18
  Israel-3-13
  Jeremiah-2
  John-4-26-27
  Joshua-2-4-9-27-
    28-20-22-24
  Levi-26
  Luke-13
  Major-10-21
  Sally-2
  Sarah-13
  William-7-9
TRADER-Richard-23
TRUITT-Eli-13
  George-10-19
  John-3
  Mary-19
  Outten-5
  Samuel-18-19
  William-13-18
TUBBS-Leviner-8
TULL-Ann-15
  Benjamin-2
  James-2
  John-12
  Jonathan-2
  Leah-2

UNDRILL-Esther-12
  William-4-12-21-26

VENNERTSON-William-4
VANDOME-Edward-4-14-22
VINES-William-26

WALTER-John-24
WALTON-Fisher-23
  Solomon-12
  William-23
WARREN-Annanias-6
  Thomas-6
WATERS-Patrick-12-26
  James-8
  Sarah-7
WEBB-Hanner-9
  Sally-9
WHALEY-Seth-
WHARTON-Francis-8
WHITE-Barlkey-17-27
  Caleb-1
  Henry-13-14-28
  John-14
  Major-2
  William-10

WHITTINGTON-Southy-7
WILLIAMS-Esau-5-6-13-22
  James-26
  Mary-13
  Nancy-10
  William-4
WILLIS-William-7
WILLITT-Henry-4
WILSON-James-7-21
WIMBROW-Leah-22
WRIGHT-Mary-20
  John-12-18-22

YOUNG-Bayley-2

Other Books by the author:

Land Records of Somerset County, Maryland
Rent Rolls of Somerset County, Maryland, 1663-1723
Somerset County Will Books. Liber EB1, 1788-1799
Somerset County Will Books. Liber WK, 1777-1788
Somerset County Will Books. 1748-1749
Worcester Will Books, Liber JW4. 1769-1783
Worcester Will Books, Liber JW, 1790-1799
Worcester Will Books, Liber JBR. 1799-1803
Worcester Will Books, Liber JBR. 1803-1806
Worcester Will Books, Liber MH. 1806-1813
Worcester Will Books, Liber MH. 1813-1822
Worcester Will Books, Liber MH. 1822-1833
Worcester County, Maryland, Wills, Liber LPS. 1834-1851
Worcester County, Maryland, 1850 Census
Maryland Mortality Schedule: 1850 and 1860
Land Records Wicomico County, Maryland
Land Records Worcester County, Maryland
Somerset County, Maryland, Will Book EB23 1800-1820
Somerset County, Maryland, Will Books JP4 1820-1837
Somerset County, Maryland, Will Books JP5 1837-1859
Parish of Somerset: Records of Somerset County, Maryland
Stepney Parish Records of Somerset County, Maryland
Cemetery Records of Somerset County, Maryland
Cemetery Records Worcester County, Maryland

www.ingramcontent.com/pod-product-compliance
Lightning Source LLC
Chambersburg PA
CBHW061518040426
42450CB00008B/1686